Planning your kitchen

José and Michael Manser

D1636913

a Design Centre book

Printed in England

Planning your kitchen
First edition published 1976
A Design Centre book published by
Design Council 28 Haymarket
London SWlY 4SU

Designed by Anne Fisher
Kitchen drawings by Jan Browne
Printed and bound by Martin Cadbury
Limited Hylton Road Worcester
WR2 5JU

ISBN O 85072 020 6
© Design Council 1976

Contents

Introduction

Nobody can put a finger on the date when primitive man stepped comfortably ahead of all the other animals in sophistication and began to heat his food. Almost certainly it was an accident —a lump of meat fell into the fire around which the meal was being eaten and what was thought to have been lost was retrieved better and tastier than before.

It is clearly a big step from this point to cordon bleu cooking and plastics work tops, but for countless years the act of heating food became inextricably mixed with the idea of the hearth as the emotional centre of the home. At first the open fire was the source of heat and food and formed the pivot around which primitive life revolved. As society developed, the source of heat became divided and part of it was created solely for the preparation of meals so that an embryonic kitchen was formed. Gradually the kitchen became a room of special character, sometimes still the spiritual centre of the home, sometimes exotic or picturesque, sometimes neglected and occupied solely by servants.

The ancient Egyptians, with their custom of giving banquets, have provided archaeologists with the first traces of kitchen utensils as they are known today, but they were limited to simple boiling pots, cauldrons, saucepans and gridirons. The Greeks, who took an even greater delight in things visual and elegant, often made the same kinds of utensils from precious metals such as silver and gold, richly adorned with figures and decoration. In the Roman home the kitchen was an important room and, in the large villas, extremely spacious and filled with servants. It was often situated in the basement and, in many ways, was the fore-runner of the modern kitchen. Its equipment included a range, a large block of masonry with separate fire rings and a large stone carving slab. There was a sink served from a water cistern and a waste pipe leading to a drain sunk under the floor.

It is interesting to compare a Roman kitchen with the following description of a contemporary kitchen taken from Nicholson's Architectural Dictionary published in 1819. Depressingly little real progress had been made in nearly 2000 years:

'**Kitchen** (Welsh **kegin**) An apartment used for the preparation of food, and furnished with suitable accomodations and utensils for that purpose, of which the following are some of the principal. A range of grating; a smoak-jack in the chimney to turn the spits for roasting; a large screen to stand before the fire, to keep off the cold air from the articles roasting, by which means the operation is considerably accelerated; an oven, as also a copper boiler, should be constructed on one side of the fireplace and, on the other side, a large cast iron plate, fixed horizontally, on which to keep sauce and stew pans continually boiling with a uniform degree of heat; several preserving stores should be fitted up, according to the number of the family; a table, as large as the kitchen will admit of, should be constructed with a chopping block at one end. It would be impossible to enumerate the whole of the articles for culinary purposes; but, besides the above, the kitchen should also be furnished with dressers, having drawers or cupboards under them, put up in every vacant part; it should also have shelves fitted up around the sides, in order to set stew pans, sauce pans, etc out of the way. Adjoining to the kitchen ought to be a large coal cellar, for the convenient supply of the fire. The water ought to be conducted to the kitchen by means of pipes, to be drawn off by one or more cocks as may be wanted. The screen should be made of wood, and lined with tin, and fitted up with shelves, so as to hold the dishes and plates to be made hot for dinner. The copper boiler is sometimes made double, or divided, and both parts heated by the same fire; each part should be furnished with a water-cock. The kitchen table should be not less than three inches thick. If the windows do not afford a very good light, a sky-light should be placed over the table with a movable cap, so as to admit any quantity of air at pleasure.'

In the Middle Ages the Roman range seemed to get forgotten and cooking was literally done back in the fireplace. Boiling pots were hung from pothooks in the chimney and large firedogs were used to support spits on which meat was roasted. As the variety of dishes increased and the preparation of food became more elaborate—a development led in many cases by the great religious communities—so the quality of utensils improved. In the sixteenth century large copper stew pans appeared and, during the reign of Louis XIV in France, utensils of tinned iron or even silver. The kitchen stove equipped with 12-20 rings appeared in the eighteenth century and was the standard cooking device until the advent of the iron coal range.

At the beginning of the nineteenth century the equipment was still pretty basic, as the extract from Nicholson's Dictionary shows, but Victor Hugo was sufficiently carried away to write, somewhat romantically that ' This kitchen is a world and this fireplace is its sun.' By the end of the nineteenth century general urbanisation had relegated the kitchen hearth to the back areas of the house—a region peopled by underpaid and ill-considered domestic staff where mistresses, even of modest homes, seldom went.

In 1841 an American lady, Catherine Beecher, published a treatise on domestic economy in which she denounced domestic service as incompatible with democratic law. From this point, the notion of labour-saving entered the kitchen door, coinciding as it did with the sniff of working class emancipation, and a newly perceivable hazard that the wife of the house might end up watching the pots.

In 1851 the gas stove arrived in Britain and in 1862 Ferdinand Carré applied to patent an ice-making machine. In 1865 James Francis designed a machine for washing dishes and in 1895, in Chicago, the first electric cooker arrived in some lucky lady's kitchen, followed in 1910 by early electric refrigerators.

By 1912 in America, the explosion of culinary equipment and effort-saving devices was well under way, but it did not really make an impact in Europe until the mid 1930s when early laundry machines, refrigerators and streamlined cookers began to appear in prosperous middle class homes. Standard-sized kitchen cupboards began to be available about this time too and, apart from a lull in the war years, the expansion in the kitchen equipment market has continued relentlessly ever since. From being almost the least important corner of a Victorian home, which was never shown to a visitor, the modern kitchen has become an electric power-house costing far more, per square metre, than any other part of the house and a status symbol that many housewives are proud, if not eager, to show their guests.

Right: The kitchen at Cotehele House, in Cornwall, dates from the fifteenth century. Photograph J Bethell, copyright The National Trust.

Personal needs

This is not intended to be a book of rules—there are few rules about kitchen design that apply to everyone, and those are well known anyway. Instead, it will attempt to set some broad guide-lines to help you clear your own mind on the subject of planning your kitchen and to draw attention to new developments and ideas that might be helpful: in other words, to gather together every bit of information that might be useful in one small volume so that, we hope, nothing slips through the net and is overlooked.

The owner of one of the kitchens we photographed is convinced that no kitchen can be perfect—even one designed with enormous care by an architect or designer. As she points out, simply *because* such a kitchen has been planned to make use of the last inch of space, there is no leeway when mistakes or omissions are discovered. Every area is accounted for in tight planning and there is no room to slip in something that has been overlooked. We take her point, but hope that this book will help to avoid such an omission in the first place.

Back to basics
Another point we would like to stress is that, contrary to the advertisements, most kitchens do not need every aid, gadget and bit of equipment that is on the market. These have proliferated to such an extent over recent years, and have been promoted so much, that the unwary among us could be forgiven for thinking that we are deprived if we don't own everything we see in the kitchen equipment advertisements. In fact, we are not. Some families need one thing, some another. It is really a question of thinking about the life-style of your own family and, on that basis, working out what you really need to make your kitchen as comfortable and easy to run as possible.

If the brain-washing has gone too deep this can be quite a difficult process. 'A deep-freeze? Of *course* we need a deep-freeze. Everyone has one now.' Well, maybe you live in the country, have a large vegetable garden and do a great deal of entertaining. But maybe you don't. Think about it objectively. For instance, if you live close to the shops, have no access to cheap, freshly-grown fruit and vegetables and the family cook does not go out to work, the chances are that you are just wasting space and money by buying one. You are much more likely to need a refrigerator with a large deep-freeze compartment for keeping proprietary frozen foods as a convenience. The same applies to dishwashing machines. A working couple who frequently eat out and do little formal entertaining would find it hard to justify buying one, except as a status symbol. The few dishes they use daily can be washed up more quickly than it takes to write about it. This does *not* mean that we are against either deep-freezes or washing-up machines— far from it. It simply means that we suggest you work out their usefulness to you before you part with your money, and the same goes for any other item of kitchen equipment. None of it is cheap.

To give an example, look at the drawings on pages 9 and 11 which are of a kitchen owned by a middle-aged married couple. They have no children and they both work. They are not particularly well off and, as they like to spend a reasonable part of their earnings on good holidays, the theatre and concerts, they wanted to keep the amount they spent on a new kitchen in proportion when they first moved into their house. The house itself is of a type that abounds in large cities: semi-detached with a long, lean-to type addition at the back. They decided to keep some of the existing cupboards, which were solid and in good condition, and to these they added a few new ones of a simple, inexpensive make. They are not particularly keen on cooking, but they do like food of the good, fresh

English kind, so they kept the existing larder and vegetable store but only bought a small refrigerator. Their entertaining is limited, mostly consisting of another couple in for an evening meal. The refrigerator does have a largish freezer compartment at the top to make shopping easier during the week. They have no washing machine, as they use a laundry for sheets and the nearby launderette for most other things, but there is a fold-down ironing board. Even when they entertain they eat most meals in the kitchen so it had to be bright and non-clinical—hence the pretty wallpaper, the small area of tiles and the warm-looking cork floor (which has a built-in plastics finish to minimise polishing and damage). There is a small washing-up machine because they rarely eat out and their meals tend to be substantial. There is also an extractor fan above the gas cooker. This is an important piece of equipment in any kitchen and particularly in one that opens directly into the living room as this one does. Stale cooking smells are

John McConnell's kitchen in a converted Edwardian house uses simple furniture and traditional materials to good effect. The cooker on the extreme left is set into the space left by the old kitchen range.
Photograph David Cripps

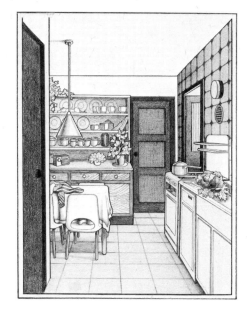

not pleasant and it is difficult always to remember to open a window and shut the door. They do not have a sink grinder waste-disposal unit as the dustbin is close to the back door. They have one sink with a drainer (more would have been extravagant in view of the dishwashing machine) and they only have a small hand-held electric mixer rather than a full-scale one as this seems to suit their type of cooking. We think they have got their priorities right.

Planning for change

All this of course presupposes a static situation where families remain the same size, ages and so on. This is obviously not normally the case, although the middle-aged couple above are unlikely to see any changes in their way of living for many years to come. For families where changes are inevitable—such as the young couple who have bought a house they intend to live in for a long time but have not yet started to have children, or the family with teenage children who will be leaving home within a few years—future changes must be kept in mind without sacrificing present comforts.

The young couple will, if they are wise, invest in a fully automatic washing machine, either with a built-in drier or with space above it on which a separate drier can sit. They will leave adequate room for a washing-up machine—the loss of cupboard space now will be more than made up for when the family arrives. And they will keep the safety of their future offspring in mind by buying a high, wall-mounted oven that cannot be opened by toddlers, rather than an all-in-one cooker that has the oven at low level (see Hilary Gelson's book on *Children about the house* in this series).

A couple with a nearly grown-up

Where space is at a premium, a remarkable amount of kitchen equipment can be fitted into a small area, but a waste disposal unit in a single sink may be inconvenient and adequate ventilation is essential.

family would do well, when planning a new kitchen, to invest in high-quality tiles, floor coverings and work surfaces that they will be able to enjoy for years to come, but to restrict the replacement of large items of equipment to absolute necessities. Their needs, as far as washing machines, ovens and refrigerators go, will probably diminish within a few years, after which time they can treat themselves to new equipment on a smaller scale.

How much space?

Another question that should be given careful thought is that of storage. Whoever said that work expands to fill the time available should have added a rider—possessions accumulate to fill their owner's cupboards. Since you are now planning a new kitchen—even if it is for the third or fourth time—this is your opportunity to make a fresh start as far as all those bits and pieces of kitchen equipment go. Here again we come to a very personal problem. If you are in the habit of giving home-cooked buffet suppers for fifty people several times a year you will certainly need more in the way of cooking utensils, crockery and cutlery than someone whose entertaining is limited to drinks before lunch or having a couple of friends in for coffee. Make a list of what you regularly use and need, another of what you use and need once or twice a year (a fish-kettle and a preserving pan are examples of such intermittently used essentials). Then look at everything that is left. Old jam jars? They have probably been hanging around 'just in case' for months and a fresh collection could quickly be made if need be. The remains of several old tea or dinner services? For all the use they have been they might as well go to a jumble sale. Flower vases that were presents and are so hideous that they will never see the light of day? Bury them. Tattered and greasy collections of recipes that repose, dusty and unconsulted, on the shelf? Chuck them out and start afresh with a single, orderly, plastics-covered folder. Two battered frying pans that you replaced some time ago but never abandoned? Oh come now!

When all this has been sorted out, you will probably find that you need perhaps one fewer cupboard than you had thought, leaving room for a larger family breakfast table, or simply space for circulation. And the cupboards you *do* keep will become more orderly and more easily cleaned. Which raises another point—open shelves. Some people like to see their saucepans ranged along a shelf in full view. They like copper jelly-moulds, potted plants and bits of decorative pottery to give their kitchen a warm, homely look. This is a perfectly valid viewpoint, even if it is not shared by the opposite faction who like everything to be neatly stored away behind closed doors. But remember that more dirt of the greasy variety collects in kitchens than in any other room in the house. Tackle it at source by ensuring that you have an adequate extractor fan fitted over your cooker and, if possible, have any shelves in a position where escaping cooking fumes do not coat them quickly in greasy dirt. Best of all, make sure that they are quickly and easily cleaned. They can be faced with plastics laminate, tiles or, if you like unpainted wood, treated with a coat of matt or gloss varnish. Gloss paint is not really as good because it is easily scratched or marked by metal objects and not nearly so easy to clean. The whole question of storage is covered more fully in a later chapter.

Also worth questioning right from the start are the accepted rules of kitchen planning. These relate to work flow, work-top heights, and a variety of other measurements that have been laid down by kitchen experts. If the cook is of well above average height, he or she is hardly likely to be comfortable with work-tops at the same level as those of a diminutive next door neighbour. Likewise a middle-aged housewife who has been used to the same work flow arrangement for the past twenty years will, if it was a reasonable one, become completely disorientated if she is forced into the strait-jacket of a completely new one—even if the experts do declare that it is the most orthodox and generally workable. It may not be for her. However, since many people will not be so fixed in their habits, it is worth recording here the classic Parker-Morris Report work sequence. This is: work surface/cooker/work surface/sink/work surface (or the same in reverse), with no obstruction or gap between sink and cooker. This has been found over the years to be a satisfactory arrangement for most people and those who have no predilections or idiosyncratic requirements could therefore do a lot worse than to incorporate it into their new kitchen plans.

Similarly, there is no need to have cupboards in all the places that are traditionally equipped with them—if you don't like them in certain places and work better without them, make your plans accordingly. One of the kitchens shown in this book belongs to a young woman who, although she is about average height, hates continually reaching up for things and is lucky enough to have a large kitchen area, so she asked her architect to keep all cupboards below work surfaces. This suits her particular needs admirably.

Different shapes and sizes

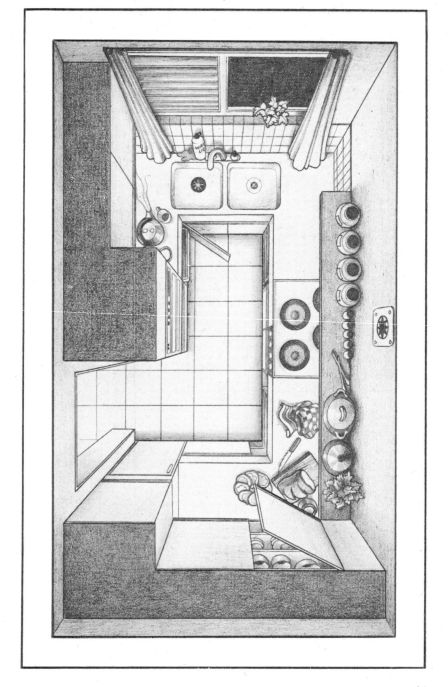

People come in different shapes and sizes, and so do their kitchens. This is yet another reason why rules for planning kitchens are difficult to lay down, let alone to implement. Too many existing factors will confuse any simple recommendations. There is one fact, though, that is worth clinging on to—any space, however small or awkward in shape, can be made into a perfectly good kitchen with the help of a certain amount of money, a lot of hard work (the amount varies in inverse proportion to the money available) and, most important of all, some very hard thinking before anything is done at all.

So don't panic at the prospect of a kitchen that is too small, too narrow or too rambling. Even before the planning stage is reached, we hope that the illustrations and descriptions of kitchens in this chapter will stimulate your thoughts and prove the point that nothing is hopeless.

Take, for example, the tiny kitchen shown in the drawings left and below. It is in a flat that has been made out of the roof area of a large London house and leads directly off the dining end of the living room. The owner, an architect, wanted to make the living room as large as possible, hence the small space allocated to the kitchen. The flat is only used during the week, the mother works and, although there are two teenage children, most of the family entertaining is done elsewhere. This little kitchen is bright, easily cleaned and suitable for cooking family meals. Everything is white—even the vinyl floor tiles—but as the floor space is minute it can be wiped over each day after breakfast washing up. Custom-made cupboards with aluminium section handles line the walls at work-top height and at eye level. The work-top is white plastics, there are fluorescent strip lights under the upper cupboards giving a good light for work surfaces, and there is a double stainless steel sink (important for large family evening meals as there is no room for a dishwasher.) There is no washing machine as the family washing is done at weekends in the country. A large refrigerator takes the place of a larder and is used for food left over from the weekend or brought up from the

country. Everything is planned to the last centimetre and the whole place is kept immaculately clean—any dirt would show instantly on the all-white surfaces. This would obviously not be a good 'family' kitchen, but for a grown-up family who are out all day and away at weekends it works exactly as it should— like a precise if somewhat impersonal machine.

Kitchens to live with

Another small kitchen is the one belonging to lawyer Bill Andreas-Jones, shown on the left. Unlike the other one, however, it forms part of the living area of his house, which has been most imaginatively opened up and transformed by architect Peter Wadley. The sitting room is at one end of the first floor area and the kitchen and dining room at the other, with a circular stair entry coming up between the two ends.

Mr Andreas-Jones is a bachelor, but he likes to entertain in the fairly small kitchen/dining area. All the kitchen part —the sink, cooker, hobs, cupboards and so on—is ranged along the window wall with a circular dining table nearby. This has a dark stained oak top for formal meals, but during cooking sessions it doubles up as a work-top when covered by a bright PVC cloth. Another non-kitchen item is an inherited eighteenth century table set to one side that has a glass-covered top and is used to hold drinks. This kitchen manages to look quite unclinical, thanks to the dark

Left: The dark stained wood surfaces used in Bill Andreas-Jones' kitchen disguise its very functional layout. See also the colour picture on page 44.
Photograph David Cripps

Right: Architect Andrew Chadwick designed this kitchen for himself in one corner of his enormous living room.
Photograph Dan McGrath

stained woodwork and other personal touches, but its appearance belies its very functional quality. For instance, the architect has installed two separate extractor fans, one over the hob and one over the sink, to cope with steam as well as cooking smells. Needless to say, there is a sink waste disposal unit (essential in a first-floor kitchen), a washing-up machine to cope with all the entertaining, and good fluorescent lighting above work surfaces. Laundry is not done at home so there is no washing machine. This is an attractive and well planned arrangement for somebody who wants or needs to have a kitchen that is an integral (and not very large) part of their living room.

Larger, more self-contained, but still part of the living room is the kitchen belonging to architect Andrew Chadwick. Mr Chadwick converted a London pub into offices for his practice, retaining the top two floors as a maisonette for himself. The living area in this case is spacious and the kitchen, which has been built in one corner of it, is 3.6 metres square. A visual and structural barrier between the kitchen and the living room is formed by specially made storage units

above and below the work surface. The drawers and cupboards at the lower level open two ways which is fine when, as here, you can see what is happening on the other side. It does *not* work if there is any possibility of somebody in the kitchen yanking out a drawer without being aware that someone in the dining room has a hand on the other side. This square kitchen set into one corner of a very large living room with virtually unbroken runs of work surface is an excellent arrangement for a young man who wants to entertain friends in an informal way. The lighting, consisting of fluorescent tubes set behind flush plastics panels in the underside of the upper storage units, is a particularly neat and effective detail.

Most people, given the choice, would prefer not to have a galley kitchen. The idea of a long, narrow room with no space for a central table for eating, and where the cook is likely to be disturbed by other members of the family wanting to get past, conjures up an awkward and inefficient picture. This need not necessarily be the case, however. A reasonably sized galley kitchen can work well, even if the family is a large one, provided that it is intelligently planned. If at all possible, this type of kitchen should never be used as a corridor—in other words, it should not have a door at each end. This is partly to avoid the problem of people pushing past the cook and partly to ensure that the cook can have at least one stretch of working surface that is U-shaped. Long runs of unbroken surface are fine, but most people find it easier to work in a position that has work surfaces on two sides so that they can group things round them. In a galley this can be arranged at one end if there is no door. Another point is that the circulation area in the middle of the room should be wide enough—say one metre—at danger points if nowhere else. This might mean that, rather than have continuous banks of cupboards each

side, there should be a gap left opposite the cooker to ensure that nobody gets jostled while lifting a casserole out of the oven or a pan off the stove. Then there is the question of where to eat. Most families eat breakfast in the kitchen at least. A galley kitchen with no room for a table presents problems, and the most satisfactory answer is often a narrow eating counter along one wall. A large family would need to have such a long counter that this would be impracticable, but a good idea is shown in the photograph below left where the wall between dining room and kitchen has been opened up with a counter running on both sides. One half of the family sits on the dining side and the other in the kitchen, with the opening doubling as a serving hatch for other meals.

Kitchens in large spaces
A very large rectangular kitchen can be just as difficult to plan. If you imagine such a room, about fifteen metres square, and think about the distances involved in walking from the sink to the refrigerator on opposite sides of the room with heavy pans of food, the snags become obvious. The aim should be to break down this large open space into smaller ones and then, in each of the smaller spaces, to group the appliances and storage cupboards that relate to one another. This will often mean building a peninsula or island unit: in effect making another wall. The photograph on page 20 shows a large, oblong kitchen. When the present owners moved in it had banked cupboards down both sides and a window over the sink on one wall, with the cooker opposite on the other. Nothing really related to anything and there was nowhere at all to eat. The new owners removed the window over the sink and put in a tall, Georgian type window at one end, near the entrance door. They removed the cupboards at this point and fitted in their kitchen table and stools. This provided a

Below: A breakfast counter acts as a divider between kitchen and dining room in this house.
Architect Peter Turnbull

pleasant eating area with a garden view, tucked away where it could not obstruct other work going on in the kitchen. A peninsula unit between this eating space and the sink and washing-up machine provided several things—a serving space for the table, with cupboards underneath for trays, breakfast cereals, kitchen crockery and so on. It also provided a work surface 'around' the sink and made a separate working part of the kitchen as distinct from the eating part. The washing machine, drier and another sink were installed at the other end of the room, where a couple of steps made another division, and this now forms the laundry section of the kitchen. Unfortunately, this kitchen does have a door at each end so that a peninsula unit was essential to provide adequate work space. Large rooms have to be broken up in this sort of way if they are to work efficiently.

Unusual shapes

When you begin to plan your kitchen, start with a measuring tape, pencil and squared paper—graph paper is ideal. Measure the available spaces carefully, draw them out on the graph paper, which makes scale drawing easier, and then begin to plan your kitchen within this framework.

Most people, as we have said, like to eat breakfast in the kitchen, but there are some who have to eat all their meals there because they have no separate dining room and others who choose to do so. This being so, the aim should be to conceal the cooking and washing areas as much as possible, but this does not necessarily mean using some large and solid screen. Often there is no room for such a thing anyway. It simply means that you should, by subtle and unobtrusive means, turn the eyes of your family or guests towards the pleasures of the table and away from the workings of the kitchen.

If the room is L-shaped, or if it has an alcove, or if it is built on two levels, then obviously it would be worth considering placing the dining table in the part that is already visually separated in this way. If nothing of the sort exists then the visual separation must be artificially created. It can be done by having an entirely different style of decoration in the two sections—cool, clinical and functional in the work area but pretty, gaily-coloured and warm-looking in the dining part. Alternatively, it can be done by having a peninsula unit between kitchen and dining area (which doubles as a serving table) and either raising the whole thing slightly, or having a raised back panel. This will effectively hide what is happening in the kitchen—certainly when the guests are sitting down. On no account have the dining area on a higher level than the kitchen, or all the tiny mishaps and messes will be seen as easily as if they were taking place on a stage.

Lighting, which is covered on page 37, is also a great deceiver. Turn off the main kitchen lights while you are eating in the well-lit dining section. Strategically placed spotlights can focus attention on some parts of the room while leaving others in merciful obscurity. It is a question of changing the emphasis of the lighting to draw attention away from the sink and the cooker. Derek Phillips' book in this series on *Planning your lighting* will give you some ideas here.

If, in spite of endless hours spent twiddling bits of paper around, measuring, re-measuring and puzzling over the space you have, you come to the conclusion that it is quite inadequate, consider an extension. Even the smallest amount of extra space can open up entirely new possibilities as far as planning goes, but this can *never* be a cheap exercise and the smaller the extension the more costly it will be, relatively speaking. But if you can afford it, if the land is available and if all other solutions are out of the question, it is worth investigating. Ken Grange, an industrial designer, added an area only 2×3 metres to his cottage, but it has given him an adequate and attractive breakfast area, as well as making the whole kitchen seem very much more spacious. Incidentally, he was obliged to build over an existing manhole but, covered in the same white tiles as the rest of the kitchen floor, it is not at all obtrusive, as you can see on page 21.

However unusual or awkward the shape of your kitchen then, don't give it up as a hopeless case. Group your requirements into areas—cooking, washing and eating—then try to match these with the space you have available. Do not be hide-bound in your thinking and try to be open-minded about how things can be arranged. That way, you may come up with something unorthodox but quite practical.

Opposite: A small eating corner has been slipped in at one end of this galley kitchen, described on pages 18–19. A tall Georgian type window was put in to give a view of the garden terrace.
Photograph Timothy Quallington

Top left and right: Two views of the trolley type floor units in Kenneth Grange's kitchen, showing the hanging storage for pots and lids. The dishwasher has been specially spray painted.

Left: The eating area in the same kitchen, which was extended over an existing drain manhole. A dished cover was used to continue the floor finish so that only the outline of the frame remains.
Photographs David Cripps

Equipment

The variety of kitchen equipment available is enormous, especially now that foreign manufacturers have successfully infiltrated our markets. Taking cookers as an example, you can choose between gas or electricity, or a combination of the two; you can have a single appliance or separate oven and hobs; you can have a cooker with one oven or two, with roasting spit or without, with a griddle or a deep frier. There is plenty of choice. The only difficulty is likely to be the length of time you have to wait for delivery.

Cookers
Gas cookers used to be preferred by some people because they were quicker and more instantly controllable than electric ones. This is not such a valid point these days, with the introduction of quick-acting electric rings, but it does still apply to ovens. Gas tends to be dirtier than electricity but it is cheaper to use at present. The choice is a personal one about which many people feel quite strongly.

The question of whether to have a separate oven and hob unit is often more difficult. Separating the two functions offers a number of advantages in addition to enabling you to make a really good, streamlined kitchen with no nasty dirt-attracting gaps between appliances. For example, you can split your options by having an electric oven and gas rings (useful in case of power cuts), or even a combination of gas and electric rings. It is also a good idea to have the oven well out of the reach of small children, as well as being at the right height for you. Twin ovens can simplify large-scale cooking operations, although this does mean twice as much cleaning. One British company has had the enterprise to introduce an electric hob unit with a fold-down stainless steel cover to provide extra work space when the rings are not in use.

Many oven interiors, both gas and electric, are now fitted with continuous-cleaning linings that burn away the dirt when the oven is in use and require only an occasional wipe over. Some electric ovens go further and are totally self-cleaning—you switch them to a very high temperature and all deposits are carbonised.

Cookers have been the subject of many recent technical innovations. In design terms though there is still much to criticise. Operating switches, auto-timers, controls, handles and hob details are often awkward and irritating to clean. Watch out for dirt-traps of this kind when you are shopping for a cooker, and for an over-abundance of shiny chrome that will always need wiping and polishing. If you are doing your own planning, remember that some cookers have doors that can be hung either on the left or the right—make sure that yours is hung opposite the area where you are most likely to place hot pans so that you don't have to edge awkwardly round the door to do so.

New developments in electric cookers include ceramic cooking surfaces where the entire hob is made of one sheet of tough, heat-resisting, opaque material with electric elements beneath. The actual cooking areas are marked on the top surface and these are the only parts that get hot. This is an interesting development, but it could be dangerous to inquisitive visitors or small children. When not in use the top can be used as general work surface.

Fan-assisted ovens, which incorporate a small fan set in the centre of a circular heating element, are a timely power-saving development. By cooking food more quickly they can save up to 25 per cent of the electricity. They also produce an even temperature so large-scale batch baking is possible.

The other main development is the microwave oven, which has been popular with the catering trade for some years and is beginning to appear on the domestic market but is still relatively expensive. It cooks dishes in a matter of seconds using high-frequency electromagnetic waves without heating the containers they are in. Speed is the main advantage but they do not brown the food so that it can look unappetising unless it is subsequently placed under a grill.

The gas industry has not produced equivalent innovations, but push-button spark ignition and automatic re-ignition are welcome refinements for gas hobs.

Refrigerators

A refrigerator is essential in any well planned kitchen if food is to be kept perfectly fresh and cool. Sizes range from 28 to 340 litres. Below about 85 litres they are really intended for use in bedsitters or caravans. The tops of some models can give extra work-space or, if floor space is limited, others are tall and slim. Because refrigerators are basically just a plain cupboard as far as the consumer is concerned, many manufacturers have unfortunately chosen to draw attention to their models by bedecking them with unnecessary and often vulgar quantities of chrome and plastics. Our advice is to choose the size you want, then look for a model that gives you the most sensibly planned interior with the simplest cabinet. Avoid dirt-collecting crevices, inside and out, and pieces of exterior trim that look as if they might peel off, chip, and be difficult to clean.

Freezers

Freezers are not an essential item, but they are extremely helpful for families who grow quantities of fruit or vegetables, live far away from the shops or, for some reason, are not able to shop regularly. They need not be kept in the kitchen—in fact the very large ones are quite overpowering—and a garage, cellar or laundry room with covered access from the kitchen, would all be suitable. According to the Electricity Council you should base your choice of size on the number in your family—55 litres for each member, plus 55 litres extra and another 30 litres for a cat or dog.

This rule could be bent more than a little, depending on how you assess your individual needs. As far as types of freezer are concerned, you can choose between a chest model, a front-opening upright type that takes up less floor space and where contents are more easily seen and reached, and a combination freezer/refrigerator which is also upright and has separate doors for each section.

Below: The Formula Four Ring Boiling Table by Belling and Company Limited

Sinks

There should ideally be three sinks in any kitchen—twin sinks for food preparation and washing-up, one of which should have a waste-disposal unit, and a third sink in the laundry area (if this is part of the kitchen) that can be used for soaking clothes, arranging flowers and so on. A point worth remembering is that one sink should be large enough to take an oven shelf—probably the largest thing you are likely to want to wash regularly. This means that it should be at least $500 \times 350mm$ and about 175mm deep. Beyond this, the final choice will vary according to the size and needs of your family and, of course, the space you have available.

For example, if you have a large, automatic dishwasher a single, large sink together with a small one fitted with a waste-disposer for scraps could well be enough. If you have no dishwasher, or only a small one, two full-size sinks plus an intermediate small one with a waste-disposal unit would be better. Stainless steel is the most popular material for sinks these days, although vitreous enamel and ceramic ones are also available. A really large, old-fashioned ceramic sink still seems to be a good choice for the laundry where its main disadvantage—the likelihood of cracks and chips caused by heavy pots and pans—will not apply.

The neatest way to install sinks is to have them set directly into a plastics or tiled work surface, without having any drainers. This will be satisfactory if there is a large dishwasher and very little washing up is done by hand—and if the joint between the sink bowl and the work-top is absolutely watertight. It will give you more space to use as a preparation area and, if there are twin sinks, the second one can be used as a draining area. On the other hand it will not work if there are large quantities of washing up, because water draining off the dishes will run all over the place and onto the floor—much better to have a combined sink and drainer unit.

Washing up

Do you need a dishwasher? The answer is almost certainly yes—ideally—although the number of households owning them is still quite small. Even if most members of the family are out all day, breakfast dishes, coffee cups, lunch and tea plates can all be tidily stacked away in the machine to await the main bulk of dishes from the evening meal. Only for a single person or a couple who eat out nearly all the time would a dishwasher seem an unnecessary extravagance—and even they might like the idea of a small, portable, four place-setting machine.

A dishwasher should obviously be located as close as possible to existing services—water supply, drainage and electricity—and it should also be close to the sink so that scraps of food can be disposed of before loading the plates. Many models are floor-standing, with a work surface top, and others fit under an existing work-top to produce a very neat and efficient effect. There are also some that can stand on a work-top and yet others that can be fixed to the wall at shoulder height. Most modern machines are front-opening and at least 550mm space should be allowed in front of a machine for loading, plus a little at the back for plumbing-in. Size again depends on the size of family and the amount of entertaining done, but you should aim to get a machine that is big enough to take the largest daily load you are likely to produce—not forgetting coffee cups, glasses, milk saucepans and all the other bits and pieces that accumulate in between meals. Do remember, though, that you will then have to have enough cutlery, crockery and saucepans to enable the machine to swallow them up during the day and still leave enough for your main evening meal.

Laundry

Have a washing machine if it is at all possible. With laundry and dry cleaning prices rising, and with more clothes being made in machine-washable fabrics, it seems a sensible piece of equipment for even a small household. This is particularly true of fully automatic machines that can complete a washing cycle with no attention and can handle a variety of different types of fabric. Some come complete with tumble heat driers in the same cabinet, and most have matching driers that can be stacked on top. The majority of washing machines are plumbed into the hot and cold water supplies and have their own built-in heaters to boost the water temperature as necessary. Some will work on cold supply only.

An alternative to the fully automatic washing machine is the less complex twin-tub, which has one tub for washing and another for spin drying. These take up more space and they are not totally automatic in that clothes have to be transferred from the washing to the spinning tub. Their capacity is also rather less—about 3kg or a little more compared with about 5.5kg for the larger automatics. On the other hand the price is lower.

Waste disposal

Two other, much less expensive items can contribute a great deal to the efficiency of the kitchen. The first is the sink grinder that will consume all your vegetable peelings, eggshells, food scraps, bones and so forth. You simply put them in the sink fitted with the grinder, turn on the tap and set the machine going. The joy of preparing a meal without constantly having to wrap up mucky bits and pieces in newspaper is something that, once experienced, you will never willingly relinquish. A waste grinder can be fitted into one of a pair of twin sinks, or into its own small third sink. It would not be ideal to install one in a single sink unit if that is all you have. Perhaps you should start a compost heap instead?

Ventilation

The second item, which is often overlooked, is an efficient extractor fan to remove fumes and steam. Not only will this keep the rest of the house free of stale food smells, but it will prevent grease-laden fumes from spoiling your freshly-decorated kitchen and keep down condensation generally. It should be set above the cooker with a wide hood to prevent even a wisp of steam escaping. If the cooker is set against an outside wall so much the better. If not, means must be found to conceal a duct to carry the fumes away to the outside. This can often be run through a cupboard, or sometimes in the space above the ceiling.

If it is impossible to install a duct of this sort, some improvement can be made by fitting a self-contained cooker hood that incorporates an activated carbon filter. This will help to remove cooking smells and steam, although it cannot provide positive ventilation in the same way as an extractor fan.

Water

Finally, for areas like London that have very hard water it is worth considering a water softener. Having soft water means that pipes do not scale, baths and basins stay much cleaner and soap lathers more easily—which means that you use less soap and detergent. In addition, soft water actually feels more gentle and pleasant and it certainly helps in cleaning and laundering.

The disadvantages are the cost of installing the softening equipment and the space that it takes up. There is also the question of maintenance. The alleged risk that drinking soft water increases the incidence of heart disease can be avoided by having a separate tap for drinking water in the kitchen that by-passes the softener.

Storage

It may seem perverse, but in the first place it is a good thing to start planning the kitchen storage by separating off the things that just should not be kept in the kitchen.

To our minds—and at the risk of offending animal-lovers—the kitchen is no place to keep cats and dogs. The kitchen is, above all, a place where food is cooked and it is a simple issue of hygiene that preparation surfaces should not be the same ones on which pets walk, lie, sniff or lick—to mention some of the more agreeable things they do. Neither is the kitchen door a good place for a cat door. Even if your own pet is immaculate, other cats soon learn about cats' doors and go visiting. Cat doors have even been used by rats.

In an ideal world, neither would dirty linen be stored or washed in the kitchen —there would be a separate laundry or utility room A good compromise is often to keep the laundry basket and the washing machine in the bathroom. It is also better to keep household cleaning equipment such as dust pans, brooms, vacuum cleaners and floor polishers out of the kitchen. Since these things are used all over the house some central cupboard would be the best place.

Shoe-cleaning equipment should be kept out of the kitchen if possible, thus avoiding the hazard of a child placing farmyard or city pavement impregnated shoe soles on kitchen table or work-top whilst wiping and polishing the uppers.

Neither is the kitchen the best place for gardening equipment—least of all fertilizers, pesticides or weed killers. Equipment just brings in the dirt and the hazards of toxic chemicals are obvious. By the same token, medicines should be locked in a bedroom or bathroom cupboard and not in the corner of a food cupboard. Clean linen, other than tea towels, should not be kept in the kitchen or it will smell of stale food. Books will tend to deteriorate if kept in the kitchen because of the humid atmosphere, so keep cookery books in a cupboard if possible. Storing petrol, oil or paraffin in the kitchen is thoroughly dangerous. At this point we start to enter the realm of bizarre uses of kitchens as storage for mopeds, outboard motors and parts of motor car—which on the face of it would never be expected to be found in a kitchen but in reality sometimes are. However, we assume that readers of this book are concerned primarily with kitchens as kitchens— unlike a couple we know who spent nine months cooking around, and eventually eating off, a home-built sailing dinghy.

Once you have disposed of the things that should not be stored in the kitchen, there will be an irreducible minimum number of items that are needed and for which space must be found. The best way to deal with these is to consider the kitchen as a series of separate activity areas and to set out what things are needed in each and the best places to keep them. The five main activity areas are: food preparation and washing up; mixing; cooking; serving; and eating. We will deal with them one by one.

Food preparation

The food preparation and washing up area generally accounts for about half the total run of fittings in an average kitchen. Ideally this area will also contain a minimum 600mm length of work surface on each side of the sink. The storage requirement will be:

Kitchen crockery
Best kept on adjustable shelves below the kitchen eating corner; at a height of between 1350–1740mm in a wall cupboard; or in a rack on the back of a wall cupboard door. Hang cups and jugs on hooks, either under the shelves of a wall cupboard or under the cupboard itself

Saucepans, colander
Stacked in pull-out racks or in deep drawer in floor unit

Knives, tin openers, strainers, peelers
In a shallow drawer below a work-top; or on a wall rack; or on a rack on the back of the door

Plastic bags, kitchen foil, string, paper
In drawers in floor unit

Tea and hand towels in current use
Have separate tea and hand towels. Keep them in a ventilated position, on towel rail or next to radiator if possible. Pull-out towel rails are available in a recess that will fit between two units

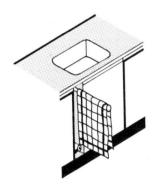

Dishwasher
As close to the sink as possible

Washing-up materials and implements
On the lowest shelf of a wall cupboard near sink; or in a floor unit below the sink; or in rack on the back of a floor unit door

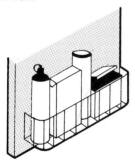

Empty jars and bottles
If not of immediate use, put them in the dustbin. Otherwise on shelves higher than 1750mm in wall cupboards

Refuse container
Near the sink in a floor unit or on the back of an adjacent floor unit door

'Wet' cleaning materials (cloths, bucket, mop)
In a floor unit near the sink, or better in the utility room or a special cleaning cupboard near the centre of the house

Food
If not kept in the larder, there should be a special area for fresh fruit and vegetables and possibly also for tea, coffee and sugar

Food mixing
In the mixing area all that is needed is as big a working surface as possible—ideally about 1000mm long—with plenty of storage space for ingredients. The storage requirement will be:

Utensils and minor appliances, mixing machines, kitchen scales
Kept ready for use at the back or in a corner of the work surface. Alternatively on a special stand or pull-out shelf at work-top level if space is at a premium

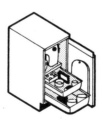 

Mixer attachments, hand-held mixers, measuring and mixing spoons, whisks, small sieves, rolling pin, pastry cutters
On a wall rack or on the back of a floor unit door; or in a floor unit; or in a deep drawer just below the work surface

Pastry board, cooling rack, large sieves, baking tins, mixing bowls
In a floor unit in deep drawers or pull-out racks. All except the heavy bowls can be kept in wall cupboards or on shelves if preferred

Food—flour, sugar, cake mix, dried fruit, seasoning, spices, preserves, all dry food
Keep these in a 'dry store' well away from cooking steam in a warm spot as close to the mixing area as possible

Cooking
This is where it all happens—where the prepared food gets cooked and where the cooking dirties the pans that go on back to the washing area. The storage requirement is, however, comparatively small. It comprises:

Frying-pans, saucepans, casseroles
Keep these in floor units near the oven and hot-plates

Fish slice, spatula, fork, ladle, spoons, skewers
Best kept on a wall rack within easy reach of the cooker

Seasonings
Keep these on a wall rack or a shallow rack on the back of a wall cupboard door

Electric kettle, coffee percolator, grinder
These need not necessarily be kept in the cooking area and can equally well sit on the work-top near the sink. They are better not kept in cupboards

Serving
The serving area is an important part of any kitchen, and a kitchen that has a special, reasonably sized surface for use in dishing-up, making last minute adjustments and serving will work much more easily than one without, as well as being safer. The act of dishing up food involves food and pans at their hottest and most hazardous— space to do it is therefore essential. If the kitchen is more than a hatch width or door opening away

from the dining room, and if there is room, this is also the best place to store a trolley—with or without a hot-plate. Perhaps the best place for an electric hot-plate is actually in the dining room, on a sideboard or side-table. The storage requirement in the serving area is as follows:

China and glassware
Keep plates and glasses on adjustable shallow shelves in a wall cupboard. Shelves 300–400mm wide are ample

Cutlery and serving spoons
These should be kept in a shallow drawer or cutlery tray in a drawer in one of the floor units

Table mats and table linen
Keep these in a separate drawer or on a shelf at eye level

Food
Leave space to keep bread (in a wooden drawer is ideal), cereals, jams and marmalade

Eating
The separate eating area in the kitchen really needs very little storage space. All you will want is a counter or table with chairs or stools, somewhere to keep the electric toaster, salt, pepper, mustard etc.

These suggestions for storage space obviously relate to the ideal kitchen. Only the largest and most elaborate kitchen could be arranged in separate areas in this way. In practice in a small kitchen the areas will be interchangeable —with the serving area doubling as a preparation area, for example. The principle is to establish where each activity is customarily carried out and and then to group the relevant storage as close at hand as possible. Although some foods should obviously be kept close to particular areas, in practice food will conveniently be kept in three main areas—the dry store, the larder and the refrigerator—with possibly a deep freeze kept elsewhere.

Food storage
There is still a strong argument for having an old-fashioned larder. If it is in a shady corner of the house, well ventilated with an air flow from bottom to top, a cold, hard floor surface and solid slate, tile or marble shelves, such a larder will make a refrigerator unnecessary for most of the year. If you have such a larder you could make do with a relatively small refrigerator, thus saving fuel costs and space, and if you have a deep freeze and a proper larder a refrigerator may not be needed at all.

These three food storage areas each have their specific uses. The dry store is exactly what its name implies—it is for storing foods that are themselves dry, and for foods that need to be kept in a dry atmosphere, such as cereals, cake mixes and sugar. The larder is for foods that need to be kept cool and ventilated, and also for use as a recovery room for foods taken from the oven or the deep freeze or refrigerator. This is where cold meat should be kept after cooking, or where frozen meat or fish is allowed to thaw out gently, and where to keep butter so that it stays spreadable. A refrigerator is for foods that actually need to be chilled—and surprisingly few really do, except in very hot weather or if they have to be kept for a long period. In most households the food travels so quickly through the front door and into the sundry digestive systems that a cool larder is quite sufficient and the refrigerator cult is a result of taste and preference as much as anything else. A lot of people now prefer chilled milk, crisp lettuce and a supply of ice.

Although the conventional idea of a larder is a fair-sized cupboard into which you walk, with shelves all round, something smaller could easily be contrived for the more modest kitchen of today. A chest-high cupboard could be cantilevered through an outside wall on the shady side of the kitchen and fitted with cold shelves, insulated walls and generous ventilation. A cupboard $1 \times 1 \times 0.5$m deep would be quite large enough for most families and would be a useful addition to the dry store and refrigerator.

Having looked at the basic storage requirements of the different parts of the kitchen, and having eliminated most of the things that should not be kept there in the first place, it is surprising how little is really needed in the way of storage space. To some extent, complicated kitchen planning is the result of expensive and unnecessary marketing—most of us are gullible prey to the 'fitment' advertisements. The one thing that a kitchen must have above all else is an abundance of work surfaces. It is, after all, a workshop. Walls *lined* with cupboards are not necessary—a commercial or industrial kitchen has very little storage space but a lot of equipment and working space. Any architect who has to inspect a block of flats or a housing estate for defects and is conscientious enough to open the kitchen drawers and cupboards is aghast at the collection of rubbish he finds. Cupboards and drawers get filled because they are there. Plan your kitchen ruthlessly, have only the storage you need and use the extra space for working in—and use the money you save by eating out! Make sure that the storage space you do have is properly arranged to suit its contents. Have adjustable shelving, racks where they save space and drawers of the right depth. The drawings on pages 32 and 33 show some examples of well divided storage spaces.

Correct heights

We have stressed the need for plenty of work surfaces, but it is most important that these should be at the right height, otherwise the cook will find every activity awkward and tiring. The chart shows the recommended fitting heights for persons of average height.

If you are very tall or short you should adjust your work surface heights accordingly. This never involves more than 50–80mm each way which can generally be added to or cut off the plinths of floor-standing units. Although the dimensions are small, the difference in working comfort is enormous.

In an ideal kitchen the surface heights should vary according to the activity. A sink unit top should be slightly higher than a preparation surface to allow for the fact that you will be reaching down into the sink itself. In theory this idea is sound, but in practice too many changes in level tend to produce a lot of disagreeable edges and corners in the work surfaces and these disrupt the work flow. If the sink unit is separated from the other work surfaces it may be a different matter. Whatever you choose to do, make sure that the general level suits the cook—there is no better way of checking this than setting up a test surface at different levels, starting with the average recommended height of 900mm, until the best level is arrived at. Having chosen the proper level it follows that the height of wall cupboards, cookers, built-in ovens and all the rest will have to be adjusted to match.

Recommended fitting heights in millimetres for persons of average height BS1195, Part 2, 1972	
Work surfaces (including cooker)	850-1000
Shelf under work surface	800- 950
Sink top	900-1050
Bottom of wall units above worktop	1350
Highest shelf for general use	1800
Top of highest unit	1950-2250

Choosing storage

Your choice of kitchen units will obviously be dictated by your pocket. If, despite what we have said above, you really want to have cupboards like wallpaper either the cost will be enormous or their quality will be pretty low. As in most other things, it pays to buy a small quantity of top quality. Kitchen cupboards get heavy use—more than any other cupboard in the house—and so it pays to select them with care. Look for the following points:

1 Good structural design. General rigidity, with well fitted joints and braced corners

2 A hard surface finish that is not easily scratched. Remember that the hand opening the door will often be wearing rings

3 Good strong handles and catches. A badly designed handle might trap your fingers or throw your knuckles against the surface and cause scratches

4 Ease of cleaning. Can you lift the doors off for cleaning? Have the drawers got removable plastics linings? Are the surfaces free from joints and fixings?

The choice of material for cupboards and floor units is a personal one. Our preference is for timber, with plastics laminate facing or simple sealing and surfacing. Metal cabinets tend to be noisy in use and the humid atmosphere in the kitchen can cause corrosion problems.

The range of cupboards on the market is enormous and many now come in 'knock-down' form ready for home erection. If anybody in the house is anything of an amateur carpenter it is fairly simple to re-vamp an old kitchen by buying drawer units, for example, and filling in the gaps between them with simpler, home-made units to match. In Ken Grange's kitchen, which we have mentioned before, he has what

is virtually a range of work-tops and a floor. As shown in the photograph on page 21, the floor cupboards all pull out on wheels like big drawers and this makes the room very easy to clean—all the fittings are pulled to one side while one half of the floor is wiped and then pushed back to deal with the remainder.

Generally speaking, the best guide for choosing functional items is to seek simplicity. If something strikes you as being so simple in design that it seems obvious and inevitable then probably it has been thought out to the last detail and will be good in use and quality.

Left: A large, quite simple, but beautifully detailed kitchen belonging to Mrs Lindy Mason, designed by John Corpe. The specially made dish rack is a traditional pattern but it has been carefully integrated with surrounding shelving. Light fittings are concealed and there is a louvred aperture in the ceiling for an extractor fan. The wooden worktop with a rounded end is also used as a dining surface. A small metal edged hole in the adjacent worktop has a fitted cover and leads direct to a refuse bin.
Photographs David Cripps

Food preparation and washing up area

This area, centred on the sink, will probably account for nearly half the total run of fitments in an average-sized kitchen. Work surfaces are needed on both sides of the sink (or sinks), with one in the form of a draining surface which should be the side furthest from the cooker. There is space for a dishwasher to the left of the drawing. Storage for crockery, pots and pans, knives and other tools, plastic bags, tea towels, empty jars, washing up materials, refuse, and some fresh food.

Serving area

This can often be combined with the cooking area, and may be omitted altogether, but a special place for dishing up food makes the process much safer and easier. Space to manoeuvre is essential. Storage for china and glassware, cutlery, serving spoons, table mats and linen, a trolley (if one is needed), and bread, as well as jam and marmalade.

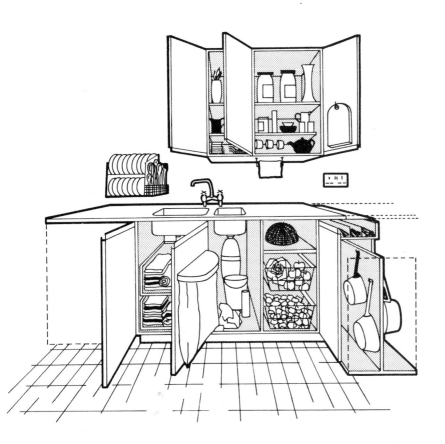

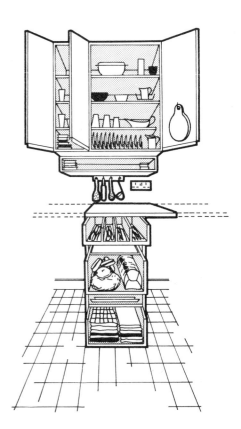

Mixing area

This area should have as large a working surface as possible, say about 1000 mm, with plenty of storage space for ingredients above it. Storage also for utensils and other appliances such as mixing machines and scales, spoons and whisks, pastry-making equipment, baking tins, and mixing bowls. Food storage for flour, sugar, seasoning, spices, preserves, and all dry food.

Cooking area

Although there is plenty of activity in this area, the storage requirement is comparatively small. Some heatproof work surface is needed each side of the cooker and a separate oven will need a similar counter beside it. Storage for frying pans, saucepans, casseroles, cooking implements, and seasonings.

Diagrams taken from Department of the Environment Design Bulletin 24 Part 2 *Spaces in the home—Kitchens and laundering spaces* HMSO 1972 Redrawn by Michael McCarthy

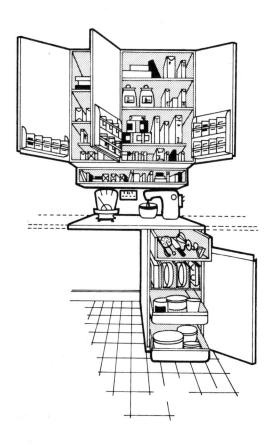

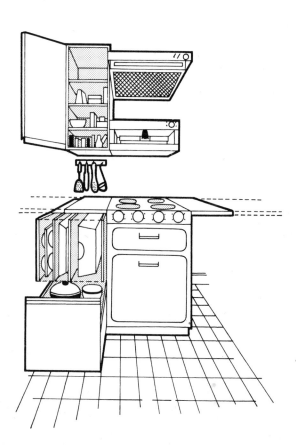

Technicalities

From a technical point of view the kitchen is the most complicated part of any house. Every service is there—electricity, gas, hot and cold water, heating, lighting, ventilation, and of course drainage. Partly because of this concentration it is also in the kitchen that there may be problems of condensation, floor loading and waterproofing—structural difficulties, in other words.

The nature of the construction of the kitchen will, to some extent, determine how it can be used and arranged. For example, the floor may be of mass concrete, resting in effect on the ground, or it may be reinforced concrete spanning foundation supports at ground level or the walls of the room below if it is above the ground. It may also be a timber-joisted floor, in which case the joists will be covered by timber boards or chipboard.

Floors

Concrete and timber floors differ in respect of the loads that they can carry, their fire resistance, and the types of floor surface that can be used on them. Concrete floors will generally support a greater point load than timber ones and, if you are thinking of installing very heavy equipment—such as an oil-fired stove or a very large electric cooker—you should check that the floor is up to the weight if it is made of timber. This is particularly important if there is going to be a row of heavy items. A large cooker might be next to a big deep freeze or refrigerator and their combined weight would then be considerable—almost certainly not too much for a concrete floor, but possibly too great for timber.

The next point to consider, if you are thinking of installing a solid fuel cooker or central heating boiler, is the fire risk involved. If the floor in the room is timber, the Building Regulations require that this kind of cooking or heating appliance should rest on an area of fire-proof material. Advice should be sought on each installation but, broadly speaking, there must be 125mm minimum thickness of incombustible material beneath the appliance and extending 150mm beyond its perimeter.

This can be expensive and difficult to arrange. In addition, equipment of this type will need a flue, which can give rise to further problems. A solid fuel device will require a 180 × 180mm cement-lined flue in a minimum of 115mm thick brick walls. The only difficulty here may be the length of flue required. If the kitchen is a single storey structure the flue may not be long enough to draw properly, or it may foul the windows of other, higher buildings. An oil-fired or gas-fired boiler can only use a brick flue if it has a tar-proof lining—sometimes stainless steel—or alternatively a free-standing stainless steel or asbestos flue. The simplest installation of all is the balanced flue used on some gas appliances which is, in essence, a direct vent through an outside wall.

Returning to the floor, concrete floors can be given a completely waterproof surface since, on the kind of floor spans that most kitchens involve, the concrete will be inert and practically free from measurable deflection. An impervious surface, such as quarry tiles for example, will withstand considerable water spillage and can also incorporate under-floor heating which, as low-temperature background heating, is quite suitable for a kitchen. Provided that the surface is suitably prepared there is almost no floor finish that cannot be applied to a concrete floor.

A suspended timber floor of joists and boards is more complicated. In the first place, it is more springy than concrete and deflects more under load. Surface finishes for timber must therefore be flexible—like thermoplastic tiles, linoleum, rubber or cork. All of these are thin and light materials that can be stuck down with an adhesive, but none of them other than rubber or vinyl sheet with welded seams can stand up to flooding. Not only will the floor surface probably lift if it is made too wet, but water will penetrate the sub-floor, causing ideal conditions for rot at ground floor level or damaged ceilings in rooms under first floor kitchens.

Walls and ceilings

The walls of a domestic kitchen are most likely to be of brick or concrete block construction. Generally speaking, they will be quite strong enough to support any standard fittings, such as wall cupboards, provided that these are fixed on proper wall fixings. Some internal walls may be made of timber studs with lath and plaster, in the case of older properties, or plasterboard lining. The timber studs will usually be $100 \times 50mm$ vertical members about 400mm apart, with occasional horizontal cross-studs. It is perfectly easy to fit wall cupboards onto studded walls, but you must take care to find the studs, by tapping the wall surface or probing for them with something sharp, and then screw fittings directly to them with long screws. Either type of wall can be tiled, provided that the plaster surface is sound, and it is slightly easier to recess pipes, cables, switches and other fittings into a studded wall.

Most ceilings will be of plaster, either on reinforced concrete or on timber joists. You are not likely to want to hang heavy objects from the ceiling, but bear in mind that it is much easier to insert recessed light fittings between the joists of a timber ceiling.

Condensation

Before going on to discuss other services, this seems an appropriate point to mention condensation. Most of us have, at one time or another, seen a kitchen where the walls and windows have been running with water. Without going into the physics of condensation, it occurs when moisture-laden, warm air meets a cold surface—as when you breathe on a cold window pane.

In a kitchen, quite apart from hot breath, the cooker and oven are likely to be producing steam, as are the electric kettle, the dishwasher, the kitchen hot tap and the tumble-drier. The first antidote to condensation is that the kitchen should have adequate background heating—from the central heating system if there is one. It is not a good idea to have more than background heating because all cooking generates heat and it is easy to produce stifling conditions. The next essential is a good extractor fan, positioned as close to the cooker, sink and dishwasher as possible and high up in the room. A hood over the cooker is not really enough because steam (and smells) emanate from other areas as well. A powerful, high-level fan in a central position is much better. One good arrangement is to have a ceiling duct in the joist space with a funnel extension dropping down about 300mm from the ceiling. The fan must be located at the external wall end of the duct to work efficiently and can be controlled by a remote switch near the cooker with a warning light.

The third way to combat condensation is to ensure that the kitchen is adequately insulated. The external walls are likely to be of cavity construction and this will generally provide sufficient insulation—although it can be improved by filling the cavity with plastics foam, a job for a specialist firm. If the walls are solid, it may well be worth your while to dry-line them with plasterboard fixed to rot-proofed timber battens fastened to the walls. The gaps between the battens can be filled with expanded polystyrene sheet to give greater insulation, provided that there is a sheet of polythene between the polystyrene and the plasterboard as a vapour barrier.

Lastly, check the ceiling. If there is another room above the kitchen there should be no condensation problems—unless the upper room is generally very cold. If the kitchen is in a bungalow, or if it is in a single-storey extension, you should make sure that the roof space above it is properly insulated.

If all these points are covered, condensation should be practically eliminated and the amount of moisture on kitchen windows will probably be within acceptable limits, unless you want to go to the expense of double glazing.

Drainage and other services
The normal drainage from a domestic kitchen will consist of a 50mm waste pipe. This should fall to the main drainage at a good gradient so that waste flows swiftly and lumps of food are kept in suspension and do not drop to the bottom of the pipe and form obstructions. Each sink should be provided with a waste trap that can be unscrewed by hand and cleaned from time to time, and each separate appliance, such as a washing machine, should be connected to the waste with an access cap above the connexion to facilitate rodding in case of a blockage.

The kitchen will need to be supplied with hot, cold and drinking water—the latter at mains pressure. It may be that the cold supply from a tank in the roof can be omitted, in which case drinking water from the mains will have to be used to supply kitchen appliances. Some machines, however, will not operate on mains pressure as it is too high. The thing that cannot be omitted under any circumstances is the mains supply to the kitchen tap for cooking and drinking. If you are installing new plumbing in a kitchen it is worth fitting a separate stop-cock in the supply to each tap and appliance so that they can be disconnected or re-washered easily without draining the whole system. Stop-cocks can also be used to reduce water pressure at the taps if it proves excessive. It is much neater to conceal

pipe runs if possible, but they must be accessible in case of leaks. The most convenient place is usually underneath the work-tops of floor units.

Any kitchen needs a plentiful supply of hot water. If this is not available from a central source, such as the central heating boiler, the best solution is an electric immersion storage heater. These are very efficient since all the heat generated goes straight into the water and they come in a range of sizes. If the kitchen is a very small one the heater can be located in an adjoining room.

Gas may be used to supply the cooker, central heating boiler, or water heater. Gas pipes, like water pipes, should be concealed if possible but must be accessible in a ventilated space—not chased into walls—and they should be fitted with cocks where they leave the main supply from the meter. Flexible couplings are available for cookers and these make it easier to move the equipment away from the wall for cleaning purposes. Natural 'North Sea' gas is not toxic, unlike the old 'town gas' but it is still extremely volatile and leaks must be treated with great caution.

Apart from a 30 amp electrical supply to the cooker, you will probably need to have at least six separate 13 amp power points to cope with a refrigerator, dishwasher, waste-disposal unit, electric kettle, mixer and toaster. Bear in mind that you may also want things like a coffee grinder, washing machine, tumble-drier, iron, and possibly a water storage heater. If you are starting from scratch it is a good idea to work out how many appliances you already have, or intend to get, and put in one double socket for each. It is also worth having a warning light on each socket to remind you to switch off things like toasters after use. The plugs for each appliance should be separately fused, using a fuse that is the right rating in each case. As a guide, any appliance rated above 350 watts or with a heater will require a 13 amp socket and fuse to cope with the load. Again, if you are starting from scratch, have main fuses grouped at the switch board so that one blown fuse does not put all the kitchen equipment out of action at once. One other very important point is to make quite sure that no electrical sockets or switches (including light switches) are placed within reach of the sink or other water supplies.

Lighting and heating

Lighting comes under two headings—natural and artificial. Although it is quite possible to rely entirely on artificial light in the kitchen it is not particularly desirable to do so and, after all, natural light is free.

You will need particularly good light at all the kitchen work stations—for food preparation, cooking, washing and serving. A tall window enables light to penetrate further into a room and it may not be a very expensive job to enlarge a window or make a new one to improve the lighting in a dark corner. A roof light may well be the solution in single-storey structures. One of the kitchens we have already mentioned started life as a gloomy room with a long, ugly, high metal window that faced north. The owners noticed that the sun often shone on the roof of the single-storey extension it occupied, so they had a 2×1 metre slot cut in the roof, installed a double-glazed roof light in clear plastics, and now the summer sun floods in. The internal lighting level was enormously increased and so the long, ugly window could be replaced by a tall, narrow one over the family eating corner. The result is a cheerful, bright kitchen from which one can see the garden from the kitchen table.

Artificial light in the kitchen is, in our view, best provided by fluorescent strip lights mounted under high-level cupboards so that work-tops are evenly bathed in light. Where there are no cupboards, the lights can be mounted under shallow shelves, as shown on page 15. Fluorescent lights are usually supplied with white or warm-white lamps that are relatively efficient in terms of the amount of light they produce for a given quantity of electricity. The type of light produced is, however, rather 'cold' and, although it is fine for cooking by, it does very little for the appearance of the food itself. As a general rule it is much better to dish up under the type of lighting that it will be eaten by—usually ordinary tungsten lamps. The ideal solution is to have fluorescent lights over the work surfaces, a separately switched tungsten light over the eating area, and another shining down on the serving area. Food can then be prepared and served in strong light but you can eat in the kitchen with the working lights switched off—thus concealing the wreckage of production in the rest of the room. You should also consider using one of the less efficient types of fluorescent light. These produce rather less light than the normal type, but the quality of the light is much nearer natural daylight or tungsten light. Lighting problems are covered in detail in a companion volume *Planning your lighting* by Derek Phillips.

We have already mentioned heating briefly, but you may be faced with the problem of heating the kitchen separately if there is no central heating system in the house. A kitchen heater needs to be protected and comparatively low temperature. An open element radiant electric heater is obviously a hazard unless it is mounted high up on a wall, which seems a clumsy expedient. Apart from electric skirting radiators, which may be difficult to install in sufficient quantity to give the heat required, the choice seems to lie between gas and electric convector heaters, fitted against any free wall space. Either will do the job and have controlled output, but the gas-fired type may have to be fixed to an outside wall if a flue is needed.

Safety in the kitchen

The kitchen is certainly the most dangerous room in the house. Statistics prove this, and it is worth looking in some detail at the sorts of injury to which you are most prone at the moment you set foot inside the door.

For the over 65 age group falls are the most frequent cause of injury. For the under fives suffocation is the greatest risk, and presumably polythene bags have increased this hazard. For the age groups in between, perhaps predictably, scalding is the most frequent accident.

The obvious sources of injury are from hot foods, electric hot plates, open flame gas rings, explosions from leaking gas, faulty electrical installations and scalding water. Less obvious are injuries resulting from cupboard doors left open, greasy floors, falls while trying to reach high cupboards, and cuts from knives and unseen broken glassware in washing-up water. Although the elderly and children tend to have more accidents than the rest of us, they seem to be simply more prone to the same hazards because of their worse balance and bodily control. Hilary Gelson, in her book *Children about the house* in this series, deals with the safety aspects of kitchens at some length in relation to children.

Safety by design

Most accidents can be avoided by good design, in the first place, and good housekeeping later on. At the design stage there are several fundamental principles to be considered. For example, it is most important not to have a change of level in the kitchen floor. If a change of level is unavoidable then it ought to occur where there is a change of activity —between the cooking area and the laundry area, for instance. There should never be a change of level between the cooker and the sink, or anywhere that interrupts your normal movements while cooking or preparing food. The floor surface should be as level and smooth as possible. Particular care is necessary in the case of quarry tiles or bricks that the laying is expertly done. The secret here is to start off with a level base in the first place.

The next design rule is to provide adequate space between the various fittings and to consider how each fitting will be used and how much space this will take. An example of how not to do this occurred in one kitchen that we know. It had a large and expensive chest-high oven and an equally large and expensive set of electric rings fitted conveniently near at hand in an island unit. The oven door was a pull-down flap type and it all looked splendid on paper. What actually happened was that, as the cook pulled down the oven door, she stepped back and sat on the electric rings in the island unit. Fortunately on the first occasion it happened the rings were cold and the cook escaped unscathed. It was a fairly easy fault to remedy by moving the island unit further from the oven.

This does show, however, just how difficult it is to visualise the actions of a person using a piece of equipment when drawing up a plan on paper. Obviously, hot-plates should never be installed where people can brush past and knock pans over.

All electrical switches and power points must be kept well out of reach of water sources, and they must also not be placed on the wall behind hot-plates. Bear this principle in mind when you are buying a cooker—you should be able to operate all the controls without reaching across the top of hot rings and pans. Watch out also for mixer taps with a swivel spout serving two sinks with a flat surface between them. During a busy period the water from the tap can be scalding and, if the tap is left over the flat spot between the sinks, water can splash all over the place.

You should also take care when

planning the positions of wall cupboards. They must not be close enough to a hot-plate to consitute a fire hazard, but equally they should not really be used without a corresponding floor unit to keep people from banging their heads. One family we know had a wall unit over the kitchen table. The father happened to be eating breakfast one day, sitting where one of his children usually sat, and stood up abruptly. His head and shoulder hit the underside of the cupboard which then fell off the wall. Apart from bruises, surprise and the loss of a fair amount of crockery, there was no serious damage, but it showed how what had seemed to be a good, space-saving idea at the design stage was actually rather dangerous.

Safety in practice

Although kitchens can be made reasonably safe by good planning, they have to be kept safe by good housekeeping—and good initial design can often help to make this easier. Safety habits are as easily formed as dangerous ones and it is not hard to get into the way of shutting cupboard doors and drawers, turning off taps and switches, putting sharp knives back on their racks, turning saucepan handles away from the edge of hobs, and cutting things on a proper chopping board facing away from your body. You should, of course, never put hot kettles or saucepans anywhere that they can be knocked over or that children can reach, and children should not be allowed to play on the kitchen floor while you are cooking.

Fire is an ever-present danger and you should know how to deal with it. There are several domestic fire extinguishers on the market and it is an excellent idea to keep one in the kitchen, ready for instant use. You should *never* pour water on a fat fire because this spreads the blaze like an explosion—smother the flames with a lid or a wet cloth. If an electrical implement catches fire *always* unplug it before you try to put the fire out, and always unplug electrical appliances after use. This is most important—a young couple we know went to bed late after a dinner party, leaving the dishwasher to deal with the dirty plates and glasses. In the middle of the night the husband half woke with a choking feeling. He didn't open his eyes, thinking that he was suffering from a surfeit of wine and food, and made an effort to get back to sleep. Then his wife woke up to discover that the room was full of smoke and shook him awake. They leapt out of bed and felt their way downstairs to the front door. Once outside in the brightly lit street they could see flames flickering in the kitchen. They looked at one another in consternation—only to find (with mounting panic) that they are both totally naked! Fortunately a neighbour keeping late hours saw their plight and, with commendable presence of mind, first telephoned the fire brigade and then set off with two overcoats.

The cause of the fire was the dishwasher, which had completed its work and then started quietly smouldering. The lesson is that you should not rely absolutely on automatic switches on any piece of equipment—and certainly not at night.

Special safety needs

The safety of children in the kitchen is dealt with in Hilary Gelson's book, as mentioned earlier, but the problems of older people need a special note here. Elderly people tend to be less stable physically, as well as being forgetful and not always alert or quick to react to danger. For these reasons, in our view, gas appliances should be avoided. Any naked flame can be dangerous to an old person and there is also the risk of the gas being left on unlit.

Particular care needs to be given to the arrangement of storage in a kitchen for the elderly. Their reach is reduced by not being able to stretch up to high cupboards or bend down to low ones. Neither can they lift heavy items—particularly above waist height. There are a number of general rules that should be followed when arranging a kitchen for an old person, as follows:

1 The floor should be smooth and, if possible, seamless as well as being non-slip. Linoleum, rubber or vinyl are good, especially in sheet form

2 Water heating and cooking should be by electricity, with warning lights on all socket outlets

3 There should be a high level of illumination, with lights inside cupboards if possible

4 Work-tops should be rather lower than usual and all storage should be between 450–2000mm from floor level

5 The oven should be placed so that heavy cooking pots can be carried, rather than lifted, from the work-top to the oven and back

6 Keep the kitchen layout simple—an L-shaped arrangement in one corner of the room with perhaps a free-standing island unit in the junction. The user can then stand (or sit) between the two units and use them for support. It is a good idea to have a short rail along the front edge of one worktop that can double as a handrail and towel rail.

You should bear in mind that cooking does not become less enjoyable with age, but the mechanics of the process become more difficult and need to be kept as simple as possible.

Decoration

Above: These details of the kitchen opposite show the built-in chopping board and marble pastry preparation surface. The grille below the window is for heating.

Decorating your kitchen is not something to be thought of only after everything else has been worked out—a sort of cosmetic job quite separate from the serious business of planning. On the contrary, decoration is, or should be, an integral part of the whole scheme. Wall tiles must be placed so that they line up with kitchen cupboards, wallpaper and paint colours must complement those of plastics laminates, and floor coverings must blend with work surfaces.

Your choice of colours and materials will largely depend on the type of kitchen you are aiming to create. Do you want it to be streamlined, urban and architectural or woody, countrified and homely? Is it to be simply a working machine or a meeting room for the whole family? Do you need to have a combined kitchen/dining room? Is the room going to be used by tidy people or are its owners going to leave things lying about? All these options are open to you if you are starting from scratch and all of them will have a bearing on how the kitchen is decorated. So will its aspect—whether it is north or south facing, sunny or gloomy. Lastly, and by no means least, you will have to consider how much you want to spend, not only on the initial outlay but also on the upkeep of the room. Some materials need renewing far more often than others.

Below: The kitchen belonging to Mr and Mrs Gerald Long reflects their enthusiasm for cooking. Architect Theo Crosby has combined a warm domestic appearance with equipment and scale that are almost up to commercial standards.
Photographs David Cripps

Colour

Colour is perhaps the most important element of all because it can create a mood, transform a dingy room into a bright one, and even alter apparent structural features. We have to admit to a personal obsession with white. It conveys cleanliness, brightness and efficiency to us and we would therefore find it difficult to pick any other main background colour. But this is a personal predilection and we are not so besotted with white as to be unable to see the charms of other colours—for other people.

The small kitchen shown on pages 14 and 15 is all white—white walls, white gloss paintwork, white work-tops, white tiled floor. It works well because there is an efficient extractor fan to take away fumes and because, being so tiny, every work surface, together with the floor and some of the cupboard doors, can be wiped down quickly every morning. The one-colour treatment helps to create a feeling of greater space than there actually is, whereas lots of different colours in this small area would do exactly the opposite. Because the room gets a lot of sunlight it never looks cold, bleak and unwelcoming, but the same treatment could be given to a north-facing room using perhaps a yellow or light brown colour scheme.

A gloomy kitchen would also look well with white as a background colour for the woodwork. After that, warmth and gaiety can be introduced by using appropriate colours—yellow or orange patterned blinds and tablecloth, a pale cork floor, natural pine kitchen fittings and white laminated plastics surfaces for example. And green, a colour not normally associated with warmth, can make a positive contribution in a gloomy kitchen. One such room has a great deal of white paintwork and surfaces, but the blinds are green and buff cotton, the tablecloth bold green and white patterned PVC, and there are green trays and kitchen boxes together with lots of rich, green houseplants that like the warm atmosphere and the pearly light coming from a fanlight in the roof.

Blue is another favourite kitchen colour, again because of its fresh, clean appearance which makes it a happy background for food. But avoid it like the plague if you have a north-facing or a dark kitchen as it will accentuate the bleakness. Or, if you must, use it in small quantities for accessories such as china and kitchen jars in a warm and woody kitchen scheme.

These then are the fresh colours— white, yellow, green and blue. Not at all fresh-looking, but popular nonetheless, is red, which has a rosy, warm connotation that some find agreeable for the kitchen. The old-fashioned French café style might work well in a dark kitchen with small windows—dark wooden cupboard doors, gingham curtains, tablecloths and napkins, some brightly polished copper pans on the walls and a creamy tiled floor in a Provençal pattern—and, of course, white paintwork to set it all off. An existing kitchen could be rehabilitated in this way with dark stain or paintwork giving a coherent appearance to a motley collection of undistinguished cupboards and shelves.

Strangely enough, several dark colours, which sound as though they might be a dangerous choice, can look very good indeed when used in the kitchen. Brown is one, as several kitchen cupboard manufacturers have come to realise. They now offer their units with deep brown doors and work surfaces, and these look handsome with a pale coffee-coloured floor, coffee and white wall tiles, and a brown or sharp green blind for the window. Black can also be used most effectively, especially if the kitchen is to look rather smart and double as a dining room. The kitchen on page 44 for example, which forms one end of a young bachelor's living room, has custom-built kitchen units that are stained black and give a very sophisticated, un-kitcheny look to the whole room. The funereal gloom of black laminated plastics would be overpowering, as well as making the cupboards much too obtrusive, but wood stained black in this way looks excellent. Dark green or aubergine-coloured stain would be equally good.

Do not fall into the trap of using too many colours or patterns. Of all rooms in the house, the kitchen is most likely to have constantly changing and colourful 'props'—packets, bottles, fresh vegetables, meat, pots, pans, china and recipe books. A simple, clearly stated background limited to two or three colours will be more successful than one with a larger number competing with one another to produce a discordant eyeful. And colour in the form of floor tiles, doors of units, work surfaces and wall tiles is relatively permanent—in terms of expense if nothing else. Be careful to choose these things in colours that you feel you can live with for a long time. If you want to experiment with a colour you have doubts about, do it in the form of wallpaper, curtains, blinds or paint—all of which are comparatively inexpensive to change.

Kitchen equipment—cookers, refrigerators, washing machines and the like—are usually only available in white, although you may find one or two colours and several manufacturers have flirted with the idea of refrigerators encased in imitation wood. The idea did not catch on. There is one range of gas cookers at the time of writing that has coloured doors and several manufacturers of wall-mounted ovens are nervously offering a couple of colours, but the concept has not been implemented well. The possibility of richly-coloured equipment matching or contrasting with kitchen units is an interesting one though, and some people have contrived their own in the absence of good-looking manufactured items. In his mainly white kitchen, shown on page 21, designer Ken Grange has introduced an unexpected dash of colour by having a dishwasher sprayed a deep forest green. At the very least, this approach could transform an old and dingy piece of equipment and also avoid a clinical appearance in a combined kitchen/dining room.

The sink is another place in which colour can be used. A range of vitreous-enamelled sink and drainer units has come onto the market in recent years in such good, strong colours as red, blue, green and yellow. It is becoming possible to buy coloured tap fittings too and one interesting range is imported from Denmark. Taps in red, brown, green, yellow and blue bring colour to a kitchen in a subtle and elegant way when matched with the sink or the tiles around them.

Apart from looks and durability, the main requirement for any material used in a kitchen is that it should be easy to clean. This is not necessarily the same thing as 'not showing the dirt'—any material that is too good in this respect risks getting a massive build-up of filth before it is spotted and dealt with. Materials that can be cleaned easily, on the other hand, are essential.

Right: Strong colours and dark surfaces eliminate any trace of a clinical look in the kitchen corner of this living room designed for Bill Andreas-Jones by architect Peter Wadley, of Wadley and Anthony. Photograph David Cripps

Walls

Walls can be covered with paint, paper, vinyl, wood or tiles, or any combination of these. Once again, the best results are obtained from a simple scheme. You could use tongued and grooved boarding in the dining area, for instance, with tiles and paintwork in the kitchen proper. Or you could have paper in the kitchen with some tiles around the sink and work-tops. Or you might prefer to have vinyl wall-coverings everywhere. Do not try and have a bit of everything —you will almost certainly end up with a restless-looking, uncomfortable interior.

Wallpaper is perfectly acceptable for use in a kitchen provided that there is a good extractor fan, and it is a speedy and inexpensive way to transform a dingy interior. Remember though that ordinary wallpaper is not washable and you will probably need some sort of splashback around the sink and food preparation area at least. Ceramic tiles are one obvious answer—they come in many different colours and patterns and can be fixed relatively easily by a do-it-yourself enthusiast, although the cutting in of switches, sockets and taps (with a masonry drill) takes patience and practice. Stainless steel tiles are another possibility.

Vinyl wall-coverings, although they are more expensive than paper, are a better long-term prospect in a kitchen because they can be washed clean. However, crude and inappropriate designs seem to flourish in this particular market and you may have to search carefully to avoid ending up with pink and purple daisies or orange and green stripes.

Painted walls are, in many ways, the best choice for a kitchen. Gloss paint is washable but it does tend to show every fault and dent in old plasterwork. Ordinary emulsion paints are not really washable and the removal of a dirty mark may leave an equally unsightly smudge. There are, however, many improved emulsion paints and vinyl emulsions that can be cleaned more easily and eggshell finishes are another compromise. Do not be afraid to use strong colours such as deep green or chocolate brown which, when applied with discrimination, make a good background for plain wood units and multi-coloured kitchen paraphernalia.

Tongued and grooved wooden boarding is a once-and-for-all job that gives a warm and well-furnished look, particularly to an eating area. Treated with matt or gloss varnish it can be wiped clean, although a softwood like pine can get scratched and marked if it is used in a vulnerable position.

Tiles, however decorative they may be (and some are adorned to the point of vulgarity), still have a hardening effect if they are used in large quantities. They are also expensive. The most attractive and contemporary application is to use them in small quantities behind sinks and work-tops where their ease of cleaning is a boon. Look out for some of the very simple one or two-colour designs, which are easier to live with over a long period than the more elaborate offerings. If you crave a very clinical kitchen then stainless steel tiles might fit into your scheme. But unless you are addicted to the constant wiping and polishing they need to keep them looking immaculate you are in for a hard slog.

Flooring

Some years ago a few retailers were promoting the idea of carpet in the kitchen—the carpet in question being a 'washable' synthetic from the USA. This was a frightful idea that failed to prosper. The whole point of a kitchen floor covering is that it should be comfortable to walk on (the carpet did measure up on this count), that it should strike a happy balance between showing the dirt too quickly and hiding it in an

Sandra Grant's kitchen is in an extension at the back of the house and architects Hunt, Thompson Associates have seized the opportunity to provide rooflights, which give an excellent light. The timber roof structure and fittings contrast with bright green post-formed laminated plastics work surfaces and the floor is surfaced with sealed cork tiles.
Photographs David Cripps

unhygienic manner, and that it should be instantly and easily washable.

Much more satisfactory are materials such as tiles (which can be cork, ceramic or vinyl), sheet vinyl or sheet linoleum. Sheet rubber, studded or ribbed, like that used in laboratories and factories is being used by some architects for modern interiors. And then there are such esoteric and expensive materials as marble and slate. Bricks look superb if they are well laid in the right sort of kitchen and even ordinary floorboards will make a practical and attractive floor if they are sanded and sealed.

The type of underfloor you have will affect your choice of floor covering material. If it is a solid concrete base you are not restricted in any way; if it is a suspended joist and board construction you are limited to the lighter types of tiles and sheeting. The boards must be covered with hardboard to provide a smooth base and then the cork, vinyl, rubber or other material laid on top.

Cork tiles have a number of advantages—they are warm and quiet to walk on and are hard-wearing. They should be sealed if they are used in a kitchen and they are better not used in a laundry area where a flood of water could get beneath them. Most practical are proprietary brands that have a vinyl plastics coating. A fraction of the natural look is lost, but the floor becomes very easy to keep clean. You just wipe it with a damp cloth.

Vinyl tiles share many of these characteristics and are even tougher, as well as coming in a huge variety of patterns and colours, and in various shapes. Perfectly plain vinyl floors are not the most practical as they show every crumb and mark, but washing is easy. Sheet vinyl eliminates the joins and can be obtained with a cushioned backing.

Ceramic tiles are tough (they must, of course, be laid on a perfectly solid base) but they tend to be hard on the feet. Nevertheless, they give a splendidly opulent look to a room, and if vitrified can be carried through onto an outside terrace. Steer clear of loud and strident patterns if you don't want them to glare at you morning after morning.

Quarry tiles are tough, impervious and also hard to walk on. They come in mellow colours ranging from buff and yellow through to deep red, blue, black and brown, making them one of the most appropriate and handsome kitchen floor coverings.

Linoleum is generally laid in sheet form and, although it can be bought in fine strong colours, it is not the ideal material for kitchen use. A heavy quality must be used and in this form it is hard-wearing, but it really needs polishing to look its best which, apart from the time involved, is a dangerous practice in a kitchen.

Sheet rubber, with a studded or ribbed finish, has been available in black and white for some time and new colours have come onto the market. The white version in particular looks extremely smart in a kitchen, as well as being hard-wearing and quiet to walk on. On the other hand, white does show heel marks (this applies to linoleum and vinyl as well) and black shows fluff, dust and milk stains.

Marble and slate, both of which must be laid on solid sub-floors, are expensive, but of the two slate makes the most beautiful floor, especially in its riven, non-slip form. Colours vary depending on the quarry it comes from—it can be dark green, deep grey or grey-blue, for instance. Marble has a harder quality that makes it less appealing, but it too is hard-wearing and scrubbable.

Bricks, like quarry tiles, make a splendid kitchen floor, especially for a farmhouse-type room. They must be laid on a solid sub-floor and there is a variety of classic patterns in which they can be arranged—herringbone, basket and so on. Colours vary widely and include white, yellow, grey and black as

Right: This kitchen's strong, functional appearance depends on the use of solid, traditional materials, including marble and wood for the main working surfaces. Photograph David Cripps

well as the more usual reds and browns. Price depends on quality. The finished floor can be washed, but polishing is not advisable in a kitchen for safety reasons.

If you have a plain boarded floor and cannot afford to cover it, repair any broken boards, sand the surface with a hired appliance (punch down the nail heads first), and seal it with matt polyurethane lacquer. The gaps between boards should be sealed with plastics wood filler. With a few washable cotton rugs (with non-slip underlays) at strategic points, this sort of floor helps to make a warm, homely kitchen.

Work surfaces

Work surfaces can be covered in laminated plastics, hardwood or ceramic tiles, with certain sections inset with marble or stainless steel.

Laminated plastics are reasonably priced and are probably the most easily maintained surface of all. Designs and colours are numerous, but if you want to avoid an ersatz appearance do not choose mock wood, marble, onyx or indeed mock anything else. Plain colours will show small scratches and stains more than patterns, but this hazard is probably worthwhile—especially now that there are some very subtle and attractive plain colours on the market.

A recent development is the entry of post-formed laminated plastics to the domestic market. Those curved edges that designers have been using in hotel powder rooms, luxury shops and bars can now be specified for the private kitchen. At least one British manufacturer is offering this type of surface on standard ranges of kitchen units at the time of publication, and one firm makes a plastics laminated twin drainer unit with a curved front edge and drainage grooves. And there are several firms that will undertake special one-off orders for laminated work surfaces with post-formed edges. The splendid green work-tops in the kitchen shown on page 46 are an example.

Some people love the look and feel of hardwood surfaces such as teak in a kitchen, and if you don't object to the patina of stains and marks they acquire with age it is rustic and non-clinical looking. The recommended maintenance treatment is a dose of teak oil or linseed oil rubbed into the surface periodically and this inevitably gives a tacky feel to the wood for some time afterwards. Some hardwood surfaces can be sealed with polyurethane lacquer which simplifies matters.

Ceramic tiles make a hard, good-looking surface, but they must be expertly laid to ensure that no dirt-collecting cracks develop. Other materials, while not usually suitable for covering all the work surfaces, may be incorporated in special areas. It is a good idea, for example, to have hot-plates set into a section of stainless steel surface on which hot pans can be rested, and to have a piece of marble (possibly from an old wash-stand) for pastry making if you are an addict. No work-top is totally impervious to the ravages of a sharp knife, so chopping surfaces should be in the form of separate wooden boards that can be cleaned and stacked away after use. A special plastics surface that is very resistant to heat and abrasion is available for setting into the work surface, but this does limit you to one place for all your chopping.

Two views of Alan Zoeftig's kitchen, which has a number of interesting details. Work surfaces are solid wood and marble and incorporate covered electrical sockets. A high-level shelving unit follows the line of the surface below and conceals an extractor—an important item of equipment if things on the shelves are to be kept clean.

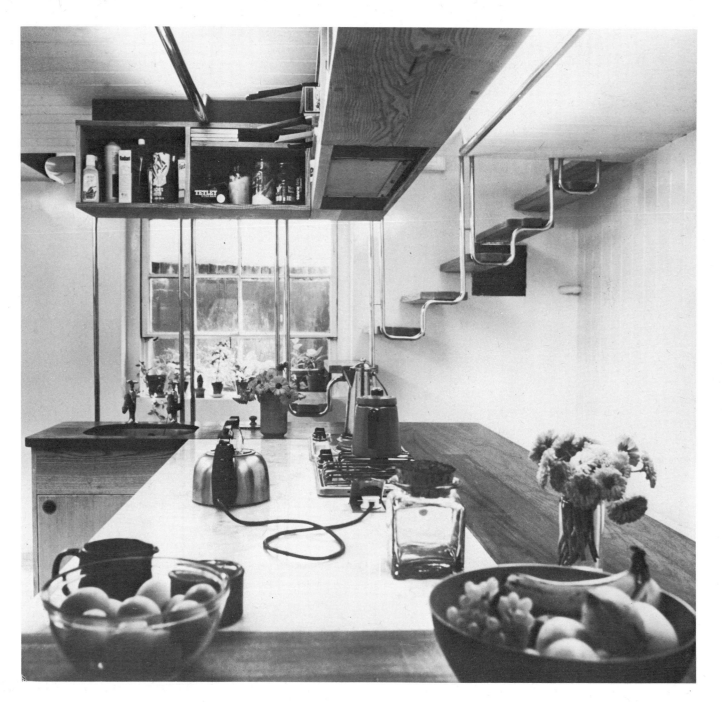

There are some interesting details in this kitchen/dining room designed by John Prizeman, notably the use of stainless steel around the actual cooking area (left), which allows hot pans to be left near the hobs, and the fact that the hobs themselves (both gas and electric) are set well back from the front edge of the work surface in the interests of safety.
Photographs John Bethel

Left: An individualistic purpose-built mushroom unit incorporating cooking and washing up equipment dominates this kitchen designed by John Prizeman. There is a larger sink unit below the window and large items of equipment are recessed into the far wall.

Three views of the large kitchen/dining room in Jenny Raworth's house show what can be achieved with quite simple equipment. The lighting, **1**, is arranged so that the spotlights for the working part of the kitchen can be dimmed independently of the decorative light above the dining table, leaving the wreckage of preparation and cooking in relative obscurity. The old pine dresser and table, **2**, contrast with the smart green kitchen units, **3**, which are in fact quite inexpensive painted whitewood. *Photographs Timothy Quallington*

Left: This spacious kitchen makes the maximum use of light from the long run of windows above sink and preparation surfaces. There are recessed fluorescent and filament lights for use after dark, and a special spotlight for the cooking area, which is surfaced in stainless steel.
Architect Michael Manser Associates
Photograph Richard Einzig

Right: An unbroken sweep of wall cupboards and floor units are combined with a curved work-top in this unusually shaped kitchen designed by John Prizeman.

Kitchens
in the future

Looking back through the ages, the nature of the food we eat and the way it has been cooked have varied comparatively little. The great traditional dishes like roast beef, shepherds pie, steak and kidney pudding and coq au vin are as popular today as they were two centuries ago and more. Only the fuels used in cooking them have changed to make the process more easily controlled and cleaner. Preparing food has become less laborious and so has clearing up after the meal. The kitchen has always been a focal point for the household and about eighty per cent of the population of Western Europe still eat nearly three quarters of their meals in the kitchen.

Until recently, as cooking became increasingly automated so kitchens became more clinical and more like hyper-clean workshops. But now, as homes become smaller and individual rooms have to be used for several purposes, the farmhouse idea of a kitchen has been revived and the room has gone back to being more of a living room for cooking, eating and sitting.

The future is likely to bring more expensive, scarcer food and less variety. Each year sees world population outstripping food supply and the underdeveloped and overpopulated nations demanding a fairer share of limited resources at the expense of the richer countries.

Energy, too, must be conserved until we learn to harness the infinite natural resources of sun, wind and water. We can grow more of our own vegetables, but it is likely that there will be less meat because of its high cost and wasteful production.

This is not necessarily a gloomy prospect—it could be an opportunity to step back to a simpler, less wasteful way of life but with the benefit of some modern facilities and methods. In the context of this kind of trend we may see an initial upsurge in solid fuel cooking, but the future will probably eventually bring almost total electric power at lowish voltages. Food storage in greater bulk and for longer periods will become increasingly important, with better segregation of deep frozen, refrigerated, cold, fruit and vegetable, and dry storage facilities. Convenience foods, as they are now known, are likely to become an increasingly expensive luxury.

As food becomes more precious, so cooking will increase in importance and skill, and we may again see the kitchen becoming the emotional centre of the home—more of a living room and less of a workshop. There will continue to be more labour saving devices, driven by lower and lower voltage current, together with innovations and developments in kitchen furniture.

We do not envisage kitchens of the future looking like flying saucers and dispensing vitamin pills like orange pips at four-hourly intervals. Food and drink and the pleasure of meal-times are too deep and natural instincts to become a mere fuelling operation. Our kitchens will change, but they won't turn into service stations.

Right: An ultra-modern—but quite practical—'kitchen' designed by John Prizeman for the London Electricity Board and used in one of the James Bond films. A single, free-standing stainless steel post carries all the necessary services, including a dishwasher, a microwave oven and a television set. Such a unit could, in fact, provide a complete packaged kitchen in the corner of a living area.

Further reading

Creating a Kitchen
Anthony Byers
Pelham, 1972

Design for Modern Living
Gerd Hatje and Peter Kaspar
Thames & Hudson, 1975

The House Book
edited by Terence Conran
Mitchell Beazley, 1974

The Kitchen Book
Nicholas Freeling
Hamish Hamilton, 1970

The Kitchen in History
Molly Harrison
Osprey, 1972

Kitchen Sense for Disabled People
of all ages
Sydney Foott
Heinemann, 1975

Kitchens, a guide to
Plan, Style and Equipment
Gail Heathwood
House & Garden
Collins, 1974

Kitchens and Dining Rooms
Penelope Gilliat
Bodley Head, 1970

Kitchens and Living-rooms
Golden Hands series
Marshall Cavendish, 1973

Kitchens Planning Notes
Design Council, 1972

Work Study in the Kitchen
Johanna Senior
Pitman, 1975

Space in the home
Department of the Environment
Design Bulletin 6
HMSO, 1968

Safety in the home
Department of the Environment
Design Bulletin 13
HMSO, 1971

Spaces in the home:
kitchens and laundering spaces
Department of the Environment
Design Bulletin 24 Part 2
HMSO, 1972

British Standard 1195: Part 2
Kitchen Fitments and Equipment
British Standards Institution, 1972

British Standard 3705
Provision of Space for
Domestic Kitchen Equipment
British Standards Institution, 1972

Useful addresses

The Design Centre
28 Haymarket
London SW1Y 4SU
01-839 8000

The Scottish Design Centre
72 St Vincent Street
Glasgow G2 5TN
041–221 6121

The Building Centre
26 Store Street
London WC1
01-637 4522

Consumers Association
14 Buckingham Street
London WC2
01-839 1222

Electrical Association for Women
25 Foubert's Place
London W1
01-437 5212

Good Housekeeping Institute
Chestergate House
Vauxhall Bridge Road
London SW1
01-834 2331

Office of Fair Trading
Chancery House
53 Chancery Lane
London WC2
01-242 2858

Electricity and Gas services and
appliances are organised locally and
details will be found in local telephone
directories

Index